YOU MEAN I HAVE TO STAND UP AND SAY SOMETHING?

YOU MEAN I HAVE TO STAND UP AND SAY SOMETHING?

JOAN DETZ

ILLUSTRATED BY DAVID MARSHALL

ATHENEUM 1986 NEW YORK

Atheneum
Macmillan Publishing Company
866 Third Avenue, New York, NY 10022
Collier Macmillan Canada, Inc.

Type set by Fisher Composition, New York City
Printed and bound by Fairfield Graphics, Fairfield, Pennsylvania
Designed by Scott Chelius

10 9 8 7 6 5 4 3 2

Library of Congress Cataloging-in-Publication Data

Detz, Joan.
You mean I have to stand up and say something.

Includes index.
SUMMARY: Describes public speaking situations,
from giving oral book reports in English class to kicking
off a fund-raising drive for a club.
1. Public speaking—Juvenile literature. [1. Public
speaking] I. Title.
PN4121.D3883   1986   808.5′1   86-3611
ISBN 0-689-31221-0

FOR MY NIECE,
MELISSA, WHO SAYS ALL SORTS
OF DELIGHTFUL THINGS

CONTENTS

YOU MEAN I HAVE TO STAND UP AND SAY SOMETHING?

1
YES, YOU HAVE TO STAND UP AND SAY SOMETHING !

Okay, so your history teacher said you have to stand up in front of the class next week and talk for ten minutes (TEN WHOLE MINUTES!) about your history project.

Or maybe your English teacher said you have to give an oral book report.

Or maybe you want to organize a community dance, and this means you have to speak to a group of parents to get their help.

In each case, you *have* to stand up and say something—whether you want to or not.

If you're like most kids, you really don't want to stand up in front of a group of people and say *anything*. In fact, you may get scared just thinking about what you'll say.

Relax. This book can help you learn to stand up and say something. In fact, with this book, you can stand up and say something good.

Something that will interest your classmates. Something that will impress your teachers. Something that will persuade your listeners.

Best of all, something you can be proud of.

But, first, let's forget about speaking assignments for a few minutes and talk about *you*.

You probably like to eat chocolate chip cookies when they're nice and warm and fresh from the oven. You probably *don't* like cleaning up the mess you made after eating those chocolate chip cookies . . . crumbs all over the kitchen floor, dirty milk glasses—you know what I mean.

But, let's face it—that's life. Some things we just *have* to do.

You may try to avoid cleaning up that cookie mess, but it's not a very good idea. Eventually, you'll *have* to do it, or your mom will have a fit, because cookie crumbs don't go away on their own.

And, neither do speaking assignments. You may use all sorts of fancy excuses to avoid that oral book report, but eventually you'll have to stand up there and say something. So, think of public speaking like eating chocolate chip cookies . . . a real-life mixture of fun parts and not-so-fun parts.

You may not like *preparing* your speech, but you'll certainly like it when your teacher gives you a good grade. Or when your classmates say you told a really funny story. Or when your audience agrees to help you with an important project.

Or when you go home and look in the mirror and say to yourself, "Hey, I did it! I stood up there and I said something and it wasn't so bad after all."

2

SEVEN
NOT VERY GOOD
EXCUSES KIDS LIKE TO
MAKE TO AVOID
GIVING A SPEECH

Have you ever made an excuse so you could avoid doing something? You must have. You're human, and humans make phony excuses all the time.

When you don't want to do your geography homework, you say Mr. McGillicudy is a silly geography teacher who wears silly ties that have silly sailboats printed all over them—and *that's* why you won't bother doing his silly geography homework.

When you don't want to go to a dentist appointment, you say you have to stay home and do "an important geography assignment." (Mr. McGillicuddy may give ridiculous homework, but it's better than going to the dentist!)

Excuses, excuses, excuses . . . we all make them all the time. The trouble is they don't really do us any good. Because even the most elaborate excuses can't change the facts. The undone geography assignment, the unkept dentist appointment—they're still there, waiting.

Now what does all this have to do with giving a speech? Well, lots of kids think they can avoid a speaking assignment if they can only come up with a good excuse. So instead of planning how to *give* a good speech, they spend all of their time planning how to *avoid* that speech.

Here are some common excuses that kids like to use to get out of a speaking assignment:

1. I don't have anything to talk about.
2. People will laugh at me.
3. I may have a sore throat that day.
4. I don't have enough time to prepare anything.
5. I'm too fat (or too skinny/too ugly/too plain) to appear in front of any group.
6. I just moved here from South Carolina, and no one will be able to understand my southern accent. (Or, I just moved here from New Hampshire, and no one will be able to understand my Yankee accent.)
7. I'd be so nervous, I'd probably drop dead from fear.

The list goes on and on. Unfortunately, these excuses aren't any good. In the end, you will have to stand up and give that speech anyway.

So instead of making excuses, it's better to face the facts. Here are the facts behind these phony excuses:

1.   I DON'T HAVE ANYTHING TO TALK ABOUT.

Sorry—this excuse just won't work. *Everyone* has something to talk about. In fact, everyone has *lots* of things to talk about.

Don't believe me? Okay, try this experiment:

Tomorrow, carry a little notepad in your pocket. Every hour—at 9 o'clock, 10 o'clock, and so on—take out that notepad and make a list of all the people you spoke to during that hour. Beside their names, write down all the things you spoke about. (Be sure to include telephone calls.)

Your list might look something like this:

7 am -8 am

• little brother—I yelled at him for spilling milk on my sweater
• mother—I asked her for permission to go camping next weekend
• plumber—he called for an appointment to fix kitchen sink

8 am -9 am

• school bus driver—he scolded me for making too much noise
• Steve—we made plans to go to the dance next Friday evening

- Mary Ellen—she invited me to a slumber party at her house

9 am -10 am

- homeroom teacher—I asked her for a library pass
- principal—I asked him why we can't have a big yard sale at the school to raise money for our football team
- art teacher—I asked her to postpone my assignment

Get the picture? Each day, you wind up speaking to dozens of people about all sorts of things. In fact, sometimes you even get into trouble because you like to talk too much!

So, you can't use the excuse that you have nothing to talk about. Even if you're shy, you still have lots of things to talk about. When you give a speech, all you have to do is pick one thing that interests you most. If you're interested in the subject, the audience will probably be interested in it, too.

2. PEOPLE WILL LAUGH AT ME.

No, people will not laugh at you. Actually, you'll get the opposite response. People will really admire you for even *trying* to give a speech. Let me explain why:

Did you know that most people would rather do anything than give a speech? And that includes grown-ups, as well as kids! In fact, one survey asked a group of adults, "What is your biggest fear?" Were they most afraid of getting sick? No. Were they most afraid of losing a job? No. Were they most afraid of dying? No.

They said they were most afraid of standing up and giving a speech!

So, don't worry about your audience laughing at you. They will be impressed because you were brave enough to stand up there and say something.

3. I MAY HAVE A SORE THROAT THAT DAY.

(And if I don't, I'll pretend that I do so I won't have to speak.)

This is a terrible excuse. Do you know what happens to kids who pretend to be sick? They grow up into adults who pretend to be sick. And there's nothing worse than a thirty-three-year-old ninny who whines about his sniffles.

Never use a fake sickness as an excuse to avoid anything.

4. I DON'T HAVE ENOUGH TIME TO PREPARE ANYTHING.

This is a blatant lie. Of course you have enough time to prepare something. There are sixty seconds in every minute. Sixty minutes in every hour. Twenty-four hours in every day. Seven days in every week. Fifty-two weeks in every year. We all have *exactly* the same amount of time to work with. The only difference is, some of us do a better job of organizing and spending our time.

In Chapter Five, I'll show you how to do a better job of organizing your time. If you follow my tips, you'll find that you can do everything you need to do . . . and more.

5. I'M TOO FAT TO APPEAR IN FRONT OF ANY GROUP.

Too fat, too skinny. Too tall, too short. Hair that's too

straight, hair that's too curly. A nose that's too big, a nose that's too small.

There's no end to the things we can worry about when we focus on our appearance—*if* we want to focus on our appearance. But, who wants to do that?

After all, you're giving a speech—*not* trying to be a beauty queen or a movie star. You should focus on making your speech interesting—*not* on making your appearance perfect.

Why? Well, two reasons:

First, there's no such thing as a perfect appearance. Even beauty queens and movie stars wish they could improve their looks.

And second, the audience is coming to hear you speak—*not* to judge you for a beauty contest. Sure, they want to see you look well-groomed and pleasant and attractive, but most of all, they want to hear you say something *interesting.*

So, focus your attention in the right place and concentrate on making your speech really interesting. If you do that, everything else will fall into place.

6. I JUST MOVED HERE FROM SOUTH CAROLINA AND NO ONE WILL UNDERSTAND MY SOUTHERN ACCENT. (OR, I JUST MOVED HERE FROM NEW HAMPSHIRE AND NO ONE WILL UNDERSTAND MY YANKEE ACCENT.)

Okay, I'll be the first to admit that America has regional dialects that take some getting used to.

Take the Carolinas, for example:

Carolinians often say "a fixin" instead of "preparing." ("I was a fixin to come to your house.")

People from the hills of Tennessee say "tommytoes" instead of "cherry tomatoes."

People from the mountains of Georgia don't put things in a "paper bag." They put things in a "poke."

Yes, this colorful southern dialect would stand out in Minnesota or Oregon or Vermont. But, it would certainly be understood. So, don't worry about having a "funny accent." People will understand you just fine.

7. I'D BE SO NERVOUS, I'D PROBABLY DROP DEAD FROM FEAR.

Well, yes, you probably *will* be a little bit nervous before you give a speech, but—no—you will not drop dead from fear.

I've taught English to hundreds of junior high students. I've written speeches for top executives in all sorts of fields. I've coached people from all kinds of backgrounds to stand up and give a speech.

And, do you know what? I've never lost anyone yet! I've *never* seen anyone drop dead from fear!

So, relax. You might be a little bit nervous, but that's okay. *Everyone* gets a little bit nervous before giving a speech. It's nothing to be embarrassed about.

In fact, I've helped many people—grown-ups, teenagers, and children—overcome their fear of public speaking. In Chapter Nine, I'll give you some tips to overcome any fears *you* might have.

3

HOW TO FIGURE OUT WHAT YOU WANT TO SAY

Okay, you've just gotten an assignment to give a five-to-ten minute speech in English class next Friday.

Now what do you do? Do you race home and start writing your speech? Do you start making lots of charts to illustrate your talk? Do you run to the library to get some facts? No! The first thing you should do is to ask yourself, "What do I really want to say?"

You know, you can't include everything in one speech. If you try to include everything, your audience will become bored and confused.

Do you remember those times when a math teacher tried to put too much material in her lesson and you got confused trying to understand all those complicated formulas?

Or, do you remember when your older brother talked too much at the dinner table and you just wished he'd shut his mouth and give you some peace and quiet?

Well, that's how your audience will feel if you try to put too much stuff in one speech.

So whenever you get a speaking assignment, start by asking yourself, "What do I really want to say?" Limit yourself to one topic. Don't try to include everything you have ever learned.

For example, suppose you must give a speech about *yourself*. Wow—that's a big topic! You can't possibly tell your audience everything about yourself in five to ten minutes—or even five to ten hours, or five to ten days.

So, start by asking yourself, "Gee, what do I really want to tell these people about me?" Make a list of all the things you could talk about:

- how you love animals and always take care of stray cats and dogs that wander into your neighborhood
- what it was like growing up in a foreign country
- how you got to be so interested in tennis
- the way you always want to try new adventures (camping, backpacking, canoeing—and now a ten-day wilderness hike with your father)

- why you've developed such a good sense of humor

See what I mean? You have *lots* of things to tell people about yourself. Now you must choose the one area that you think will be the most interesting, or the most helpful, or the most unusual.

Remember, if you try to tell the audience everything about yourself, you will just bore them or confuse them—and they won't get a good understanding of who you really are.

WHAT IF YOU CAN'T THINK OF ANYTHING TO SAY?

Can't think of anything to talk about? Don't panic. Just ask yourself, "What's the one subject that always catches my attention? What do I really care about? What topic would I like to hear more about?"

If *you're* interested in the topic of your speech, that enthusiasm will probably rub off on your audience.

Once you get a good idea for a speech, stick with it. Don't keep switching topics or trying something else. Commit yourself to that topic, and move ahead with your preparations.

And don't be too fussy about when you get your good ideas. The mystery writer Agatha Christie once said, "The best time for planning a book is while you're doing the dishes." That can also apply to speeches.

Who knows what wonderful ideas you'll get while you're doing the dishes or making your bed or walking the dog? If it's a good idea, grab it . . . and move on to the next step.

4

HOW TO FIGURE OUT WHAT YOUR AUDIENCE WANTS YOU TO SAY

don't have to tell you that people are different. No two individuals anywhere in the world are exactly alike. Even twins who look identical have their own unique qualities, their own special personalities.

Well, this also applies to groups of people. No two groups of people—no two audiences—are exactly alike. If you are going to be a good speaker, you will have to think about—you will have to analyze—the special "personality" of each audience. And you will have to plan a speech that caters to your audience's personality. Does this "audience analysis" process sound difficult? Well, it really isn't. In fact, every day of your life, you probably analyze many different audiences.

For example: You may tell your best friend about the crush you have on the new kid in math class, but you wouldn't dream of standing up in math class and telling the whole class about that same crush. (Why? Because what's an appropriate message for a close friend would be inappropriate for a roomful of classmates.)

Or, you may tell your mother that you feel really sad about the death of your pet dog, but you wouldn't tell a stranger about those sad feelings. (You know that emotions are very personal, and it wouldn't feel right to share them with strangers.)

So, you can see that you instinctively analyze many different audiences each day . . . whether you're aware of the process or not.

Let me give you another example of audience analysis.

You probably watch a lot of television, right? And you have a favorite show, the one you watch regularly each week?

Well, then, you are a member of a certain television viewing audience. That is, the people who write the script for this show think about you when they write it. The people who act in this show think about you when they act in it. And the people who advertise their products on this show think about you when they plan their advertising.

Now, of course, they don't think about you personally. Obviously, they don't know you as an individual. But, they certainly know that you—and many other young people with similar interests—are a part of their audience.

Try this simple experiment:

The next time you sit down to watch your favorite TV show, have a pencil and paper handy. Make a list of all the commercials that appear during the show. Your list might look something like this:

My Favorite Situation Comedy, Tuesday, 8-8:30PM

- toothpaste for the whole family
- a soft drink
- homestyle cookies

Now, sit down and watch a TV show that you don't normally watch—perhaps your baby brother's favorite cartoon on early Saturday morning. Make a list of all the commercials that appear on this program:

A Cartoon Show, Saturday, 7:30-8AM

- pre-sweetened cereal
- a new kind of doll
- computerized toys

Finally, sit down and watch the evening news for half an hour. Make a list of all the products that are advertised during this program:

The Nightly News, Weeknights, 6:30-7PM

- a new style of station wagon
- life insurance
- beer

Now, compare these three lists. Notice how each show advertises a different set of products? That's because each show caters to a different audience. The little kids who watch Saturday morning cartoons want one set of products; the adults who watch the evening news want another set of products.

This is an important point for you to realize, because when you give a speech, each audience will want to hear something slightly different from you.

A funny speech that would work just fine with your school's drama group might seem too silly if you gave it to a local civic group for a Columbus Day celebration.

An oral book report on the Civil War that would interest your history class might seem boring if you gave it to a school assembly who wanted to be entertained.

It's up to you to tailor your subject to your audience's needs. How can you do this? Before you begin to prepare your speech, ask yourself some basic questions about the audience:

1. WHAT'S THE SIZE OF THE AUDIENCE?

Will you be talking to a handful of people? A classroom filled with people? A whole auditorium filled with people?

Smaller groups tend to pay closer attention . . . especially if there's a teacher or principal or parent present! People in a small group hesitate to daydream or show restlessness because they're afraid of getting caught. Or they're afraid of hurting your feelings. Or they're afraid the rest of the audience will think they're bad listeners.

But bigger groups tend to daydream more, to let their thoughts drift, to fidget a bit. After all, it's easy to feel anonymous in a large group. Who can possibly tell that your mind is wandering?

So if you have to speak to a large group—say, the whole student body, or a large parent-teacher meeting—be sure to plan material that will really catch (and keep!) the audience's attention.

2. WHAT'S THE AGE RANGE OF THE AUDIENCE?

Will you be speaking to your peer group—kids your own age?

Will you be speaking to students with teachers present?

Will you be speaking only to adults—a group of teachers, perhaps, or a group of parents?

Think about these questions, and choose material that's right for the people in your particular audience.

3. WILL YOU KNOW THE PEOPLE IN THE AUDIENCE, OR WILL THEY BE STRANGERS?

When people know you really well, they often think they can predict how you will behave. Suppose you have a reputation for being a very serious person. If you suddenly decide to give a funny speech, your audience might be so startled that they won't know how to respond. You will have to develop your humor very carefully so they can feel comfortable with your speech.

On the other hand, when people don't know anything about you—when you're talking to a group of total strangers—you must be quite careful about first impressions. The way you appear in your speech is the way these people will remember you.

If you make a funny speech, the audience will remember you as a funny person. If you make a boring speech, the audience will remember you as a boring person. If you make an interesting speech, the audience will remember you as an interesting person.

4. WHY ARE THESE PEOPLE COMING TO HEAR YOU SPEAK?

Will the audience be there because they're really interested in your subject, or did someone—maybe a teacher or a parent—force them to go?

If the audience is really interested in your subject, or if they came to hear you because they really like you, they will be much more tolerant of your presentation.

But, if you're talking to a "captive" audience—if they're stuck in a classroom or forced to attend an assembly program—they may have a "show me" attitude. You will have to work harder to make them listen to your message.

5. WHAT DOES YOUR AUDIENCE ALREADY KNOW ABOUT THIS SUBJECT?

Suppose you want to persuade school administrators to start a girls' basketball team. Has anyone else tried to persuade them on this subject? What did the other person say to them? Was that person's information accurate?

How to Figure Out Your Audience . . . **19**

6. HOW OFTEN DOES THIS AUDIENCE GET TOGETHER?

Does the audience meet regularly? (For example: A science class that meets every afternoon at 1:30? A parent-teacher organization that meets once a month? A church youth group that meets every Saturday evening?)

Or is this audience getting together just to hear you present your ideas? If so, you'd better make doubly sure you don't waste their time.

7. WHERE WILL THIS AUDIENCE MEET?

Will the location of your speech really matter? Yes. Let me give you an example.

Think, just for a minute, about your table manners. When you eat dinner at home with your family, you probably eat a certain way—that is, you follow certain basic "rules" of behavior in your household. But when you go on an outdoor picnic, you eat differently—you pick up the picnic foods with your fingers, you talk louder, you laugh more. In short, you can be more relaxed at a picnic.

When you go to a relative's house for a holiday dinner, you're probably on better behavior than you would be at your own home. To start with, you're probably wearing newer, cleaner clothes. You've been warned against running around, yelling, roughhousing. And you know—you *know*—that this is the wrong place to act up.

What might be perfectly acceptable at an outdoor picnic will get you in trouble at your aunt's home. So, you've learned to make your table manners fit the location.

Now, you must also learn to make your speech fit the location.

For example:

• _in your classroom_ Project your voice so everyone can hear you; make sure that any posters you use are big enough to be seen from the back of the room (which, by the way, is probably where the teacher will sit to evaluate you!).

• _in a section of the library_ Keep your voice low so you don't disturb other people in the library.

• _in a large auditorium_ You will probably need to use a microphone (be sure to test this equipment in advance); you might also want to rope off the back rows of the auditorium so the audience will be forced to take seats down front.

• _on an outdoor platform_ You must be prepared for lots of background noise (honking car horns, perhaps, or squealing brakes); you must also be prepared for a sudden gust of wind, which could cause your notes to fly away; you should also be prepared for a summertime thunderstorm, which could force you to wrap up your speech early and flee for cover.

8. WHEN WILL THE AUDIENCE MEET?

Again, be specific. Think about when—_exactly_ when—you will give your speech:

• at an early-morning assembly program that meets before the start of the school day?

You have to be especially interesting when you speak at an early-morning program. Why? Because the audience had to get up extra-early to get to that program. Maybe they even had to skip breakfast to get there on time! Anyway, if your speech isn't really interesting, the audience will become annoyed. They will mumble to themselves, "Why did this jerk waste our time with such a boring speech?"

Also, you have to be especially brief when you speak early in the morning. Why? Because your audience still faces a whole day's work ahead of them. Teachers, for example, may still have some papers to grade before the start of their day's schedule. Parents may have to rush off to work. Fellow students may have even more important things to do—like passing notes to their friends in the hallway! If your speech runs too long, they will resent you for interfering with their personal schedules.

• on a panel that meets after school?

Suppose you are one of four students to speak on a panel. Find out whether you'll speak first or last. Panel presentations often run behind schedule, and if you are the last speaker, you might feel squeezed for time. Prevent this by asking the moderator of the panel to set up time limits for each participant.

• before lunch?

Put yourself in the audience's place. It's 11:30 in the morning. They're hungry. They want to eat lunch. They're restless. They want to go to the cafeteria and visit with their friends. They do *not* want to listen to a long speech. They do *not* want to sit in that classroom one minute longer than they have to. So, keep your speech brief—and let them get to lunch on time!

- during the last class of the day?

Remember that your listeners have been in school for about six hours. They are getting tired. Maybe they are getting bored. Make sure your speech doesn't make them any more tired or bored than they already are! Try to make your speech as lively and interesting as possible. Use funny stories, real-life examples, unusual statistics—anything to keep your audience awake and interested in your message.

- at 8pm, as the after-dinner speaker at an awards banquet?

A banquet audience has been eating and talking (maybe even drinking) for several hours. They will be in a good mood, and they will want to stay in a good mood. Don't ruin their fun with a speech that's too long or too serious.

SHOULD YOU ASK FOR A PARTICULAR TIME SLOT?

Suppose you're the captain of the basketball team, and your coach asks you to speak at the annual sports awards dinner. You learn that twenty fellow athletes will receive awards that night, and you're afraid the audience will be too restless to listen to your speech after sitting through all those award presentations. What should you do?

Speak to the person who invited you to speak—in this case, your coach. Ask about the schedule for that evening's events. If you are tentatively scheduled to speak *after* all those awards are given out, ask the coach to rethink the schedule. Say that you would be able to do a better job—and that the audience would enjoy you more—if you spoke *before* the award presentations. Explain your reasoning.

Of course, he may not take your suggestion. But, if you don't ask for a good speaking slot, you probably won't get one. So be assertive. Ask.

A CAUTION ABOUT DANCES

Sometime, you might be asked to speak at a school dance—perhaps to introduce a DJ, or welcome a special guest of honor, or spearhead a fundraising drive.

Know what you're up against. Kids who are at a dance want to have a good time. They do not like it when you turn off the music and make long-winded speeches. If you must speak, keep it short.

Take Franklin Delano Roosevelt's advice: "Be brief, be sincere, be seated."

5

HOW TO GET
THE INFORMATION
YOU NEED

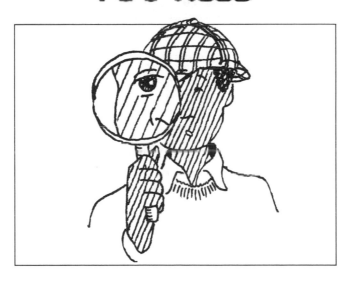

Okay, now you've thought about the subject you want to talk about. You've also thought about your audience and what they want (or need!) to hear from you. Now it's time to do some research for your speech. Where do you go first to find the information you need? Nowhere!

Nowhere? That's right. You don't need to go anywhere right now. Just sit down and think.

You know, your best information source is always your own head. Ask yourself, "What do I already know about this subject?" You'll be surprised at how much information you have right there in your own head!

Suppose you're asked to talk about your science project. Well, you've worked on that project for weeks, so you already have more than enough information. In fact, you know more about that particular project than anyone else in your class! All you have to do is organize your information and make it interesting for your classmates.

Or suppose you're asked to give an oral book report for English class. Well, since you've read the book, you already have plenty of raw material. All you have to do is take that raw material and make it interesting for your classmates.

Or suppose you're asked to give a fund-raising speech so your school can buy new band uniforms. Well, if you're involved in band, you already know a lot about the band's need for new uniforms. Even if you don't know all the details, at least you can contact the band leader to get that missing information.

You don't have to spend hours in the library investigating any of these presentations. Just think about what you already know about your subject and write down whatever information you have—a list of important facts, opinions, examples, et cetera.

Don't worry about organization at this point. Just make some rough notes. Your notes might look something like this:

FUND RAISING SPEECH TO
BUY NEW BAND UNIFORMS

information I already know:

1. band has 73 members
2. bandleader got the city's "teacher of the year" award last year
3. band members meet twice a week during school hours
4. band members meet twice a week after school hours (on their own time)
5. band members practice at least five hours each week at home
6. parents of band members must provide transportation to and from all band rehearsals and performances
7. band uniforms are old and ragged-looking—it's embarrassing for players to wear these old uniforms to parades

Now, look at that list carefully. What information is missing? What information do you need if you want to convince people to give money to the band?

Think like a newspaper reporter. Newspaper reporters ask certain basic questions whenever they research a story. They ask "The Five W's"—Who? What? Where? When? Why? And then they ask "The Big H's"—How? How long? How much?

Apply these basic questions to the research for *your* speech:

• *Who* will be responsible for choosing the new uniforms?
• *What* will we do with the old ones?

- *Where* will we go to buy the new uniforms?
- *When* should we buy them?
- *Why* can't we wait a few years to get new uniforms?
- *How* will we do our fund raising?
- *How long* will the new uniforms last?
- *How much* money will everything cost?

See what I mean? If you ask questions like a newspaper reporter, you will get some good answers.

WHO CAN YOU ASK?

If you want to get the right information, you have to ask the right people. For this "band uniform" speech, you could interview your bandleader or your school principal . . . or *both* of them! They should be able to give you lots of basic information.

What's the best way to do an interview? Here are eight practical tips:

1. Always make an appointment for an interview. Try saying something like, "Mrs. Jones, I'm working on a speech to raise money for band uniforms, and I have a few questions about the band's budget. Could you find ten minutes to talk with me this week? I'd really appreciate any information you could give me." (Since you are asking a favor of Mrs. Jones, let *her* choose the time for the appointment.)

2. Never just drop in on people and assume they will have the time to answer your questions. People have busy schedules, and it would be rude for you to show up unannounced and expect an interview. (Look at it this way: You don't like it when people drop in on you and interrupt your favorite TV show, or your supper, or your visit with a good friend. So treat others the same way you like to be treated.)

3. Write out your questions before you go to the interview. Keep them short and simple.

4. Take a notepad and pencil to the interview, and take good notes. Be sure to write legibly. (It's embarrassing if you can't read your own handwriting when you get back home!)

5. If you are confused about something, speak up. Say, "Excuse me, Mrs. Jones, but I missed that number. Did you say 'fifteen dollars' or 'fifty dollars?'" (Never be embarrassed to double-check your information. It's better to correct a little mistake before it becomes a big mistake!)

6. If it's a long interview, use a tape recorder. Always ask the person's permission before you turn it on. For example, "I want to be sure I don't miss any information, so I brought along a tape recorder. That way I can listen to it at home and make sure I got everything right. Is it okay with you if I use it?" (Most people will say, "yes." But if the person says, "no," then you have to respect her answer.)

7. Even if you use a tape recorder, be sure to take notes. When Mrs. Jones sees you using your pen or pencil, she will forget about the tape recorder and relax! (Also, tape recorders sometimes fail. You should always have written notes as a backup.)

8. Finish the interview on schedule. If you asked for ten minutes, then close your notebook after ten minutes and thank her for giving you an interview. (In many cases, the person will say, "Oh, there's no need to rush off. If you have any more questions, you can stay." You will often get your best information at the end of an interview, so keep taking notes and keep running your tape recorder. It's okay for the interviewee to relax at the end of your session, but you have to stay alert and keep right on working!)

A WORD OF CAUTION

Whenever you ask someone's permission to record an interview, you must treat that tape recording with respect. You—AND ONLY YOU—should listen to that material. Don't take the tape to school and play it for your friends in the cafeteria so you can all laugh about how weird Mrs. Jones sounds. If Mrs. Jones ever found out about that, you would lose her respect—and probably her cooperation on the project.

HOW TO MANAGE
YOUR TIME

As you start to research your speech, you might begin to feel overwhelmed. You might say to yourself, "Where am I going to get the time to do all this stuff?"

Relax. You already have all the time you need. You have twenty-four hours in your day (the same as everybody else), and that's *plenty* of time—If You Manage it Well.

How can you learn to manage your time? Well, start by taking a look at how you spend your day. Prepare a time chart and write down all the things you do.

Record this chart for a couple of days and see if you notice any patterns in the way you spend your time.

Here are some common time-wasters:

• Do you oversleep every morning?

- Do you lose time hunting for your books before you go to school?
- Do you lose time trying to decide what clothing to wear?
- Do you hang out with your friends every day after school?
- Do you watch TV as soon as you get home from school?
- Do you talk on the telephone every night after supper?

If so, think about ways you can adjust your schedule to get more time. Maybe you can limit your phone calls to ten minutes. Maybe you can skip going to the local hangout one day a week. Maybe you can buy a new alarm clock and set it one-half hour early. Maybe you can turn off the TV an hour before you go to bed—and use that extra time to work on special projects.

Remember: The time you save really adds up. If you redirect just thirty minutes each day, you'll have an extra one hundred eighty hours each year. If you redirect an hour of your time each day, you'll have an extra 365 hours each year.

As Lord Chesterfield said in a letter to his son way back in 1746: "Take care of the minutes, for the hours will take care of themselves."

HOW TO DO RESEARCH
IN A LIBRARY

There are about one hundred thousand libraries in America, with more than two billion books in them. Where should you start?

Start at your school library. Tell your librarian about the research you want to do for your speech, and ask for suggestions. (Again, don't assume that librarians have nothing else to do but sit around and wait for your request. Librarians are plenty busy. They may have to ask you to come back later—when they'll have more time to give you individual help.)

Most reference books cannot be taken from the library because they are very expensive, and libraries can't risk losing them. So always take a notebook and pencil to the library and allow yourself plenty of time to copy information from the books. (In other words, don't go to the library at noon when you know you're meeting someone special for lunch in fifteen minutes!)

If you borrow books from the library, be considerate—return them on time.

SOME BOOKS THAT WILL HELP YOU

Here are some books that will help you give better speeches, funnier speeches, more interesting speeches. You should be able to find most of them in your school library or your community library. If not, ask the librarian to order a copy.

Anecdotes, Statistics and Facts

Isaac Asimov's Book of Facts, by Isaac Asimov (Grosset & Dunlap, 1979)

> This book is lots of fun to read. In fact, you will probably enjoy looking at it even if you don't have any research to do. It gives you three thousand unusual bits of information in almost one hundred different categories (ranging from transportation to military secrets to fossils).

The World Almanac and Book of Facts, edited by Hana
U. Lane (Newspaper Enterprise Association, yearly).

This is the best American book on facts. Since
it's only $4.95 in paperback, you might want to get
a copy to keep at home. It has almost one thousand
pages. It also has an excellent index that makes it
easy to find anything you're looking for . . . information about sports, politics, health, movies, geography, whatever.

A Third Treasury of the Familiar, edited by Ralph L.
Woods (Macmillan, 1980)

This book is also fun to browse through . . . especially if you like bits of gossip about historical
figures. For example, it tells why William
Faulkner—one of our country's greatest writers—
quit his job as postmaster: "As long as I live under
the capitalistic system, I expect to have my life in-
fluenced by the demands of moneyed people. But I
will be damned if I propose to be at the beck and
call of every itinerant scoundrel who has two cents
to invest in a postage stamp. This, sir, is my resigna-
tion."

Quotations

Peter's Quotations: Ideas For Our Time, edited by Dr.
Lawrence J. Peter (Bantam, 1980)

This is a great collection of quotations. You'll
find funny quotes from Woody Allen, inspirational
quotes from Martin Luther, business quotes from
Henry Ford . . . and thousands of others. This book
is sold in paperback for only $3.50—you might
want to get a copy to use at home. It will help you
throughout high school and even college.

The Penguin Dictionary of Proverbs, edited by Rosaline Fergusson (Penguin, 1983)

This book has about 6,000 proverbs, all organized by theme. For example, the "eating" category has dozens of different proverbs from around the world. Some are funny: "Garlic makes a man wink, drink and stink." Some are based on the Bible: "Man cannot live by bread alone." Some offer sound advice: "Oysters are only in season in the R months." (The "R months" are those that have the letter "R" in their name. Notice that the summer months of May, June, July and August don't have an "R" in their names. In the old days, before refrigeration, it would have been risky to eat oysters during the summer months because they would have spoiled.)

The City: A Dictionary of Quotable Thought on Cities and Urban Life, edited by James Clapp. (Center for Urban Policy Research, 1984)

Do you need a quotation about Rome? Paris? London? How about smaller cities, like Toledo, Ohio; Newark, New Jersey; Hollywood, California? You can find quotations about all of these places (and more!) in this book.

Are you doing a special project for geography class, or social studies? This book can also give you some wonderful quotations about air pollution, sanitation, earthquakes, fog, slums, subways . . . and lots of other topics.

General Reference

The Address Book: How to Reach Anyone Who's Anyone, by Michael Levine (Putnam, 1984)

Have you ever wanted to write a fan letter to

someone famous—perhaps a baseball star or an actress or a rock-and-roll singer?

Or have you ever wanted to write a letter of complaint to the president of a big company?

Well, then, you will love *The Address Book.* This book gives you direct access to more than three thousand celebrities, corporate executives and other VIP's. Just look up the person's name, and you'll find a mailing address. (Sorry, no telephone numbers.)

Encyclopedia of Associations, edited by Denise S. Akey (Gale Research Company, yearly)

This is a very important, very big, and very expensive reference book. If your school library doesn't have it, try your community library. Ask the librarian to show it to you and to explain how it is organized.

What makes this book so big? Well, it describes about seventeen thousand business and professional associations across America. That's seventeen *thousand!* And it gives you the names and telephone numbers of people in those associations who can give you up-to-date information on thousands of topics.

Suppose you're preparing a speech for health class. Well, you can look in this book and find the names of dozens of health-care professionals who would be willing to give you information. Write to them, identify yourself, and ask for any material they can give you on diabetes, cancer, heart attacks—whatever you're speaking about.

Facts About the Presidents, by Joseph Nathan Kane (H. W. Wilson Company, 1978)

Do you have to give a speech in history class about John Fitzgerald Kennedy, or any of the other presidents? Then look at this book. It's easy and quick to use.

You'll get all the biographical details of Kennedy's life (birthdate, education, religion, marriage, children, and much more).

And you'll learn about what was happening in the world during his presidency: the first live television press conference, the Berlin Wall, the first U.S. astronaut in orbit.

The American Book of Days, edited by Jane Hatch (H. W. Wilson Company, 1978)

Are you giving a speech on October twenty-third? Then turn to this reference book and find out what happened on that date in history. Audiences love to "turn back the clock" and think about things that happened on a particular date ten, fifty, or even one hundred years ago.

Hit Songs, compiled by the American Society of Composers, Authors & Publishers (ASCAP)

This handy book lists all the hit songs of the twentieth century.

Suppose you're doing a history project on World War II. You can look in this book to find out the hit songs of that era: "Don't Sit Under the Apple Tree With Anyone Else But Me," or "Oh, What a Beautiful Mornin'." Maybe your librarian can locate records of these songs for you to play when you present your project. The songs will help set the mood and give your classmates a better appreciation of life in America during the war.

You can get a free copy by writing to American Society of Composers, Authors & Publishers, One Lincoln Plaza, New York, NY 10023.

6

HOW TO ORGANIZE YOUR MATERIAL

Okay, you've done enough thinking. Now you have to sit down and put the whole speech together.

If you want a good speech, you should make it simple and short. If you want a great speech, you should make it even simpler and shorter.

Here's the secret for organizing a successful speech:

- Tell them what you're going to tell them.
- Tell them.
- Tell them what you've told them.

And then *stop!*

TELL THEM WHAT YOU'RE GOING TO TELL THEM: THE INTRODUCTION

This is the hardest part of any speech. If you don't hook your listeners right away, if you don't grab their attention within the first thirty seconds, if you don't come across as an interesting person—well, your speech will probably flop.

I'm sorry if that sounds scary, but it's the truth. If you bore your audience right at the beginning, they just won't bother listening.

And, who could blame them? If you were in the audience, would you want to listen to a dry, boring speech? Of course not!

So, come up with a good introduction—one that will really get the audience's attention.

Here are some good ways to start a speech:

Use a Powerful Statistic.

Suppose you're talking to a parent-teacher group about alcohol abuse in the schools. You could open with something like this:

"Every day in this country, at least one thousand kids come to school drunk. Could one of them be *your* child?"

Tell an Anecdote About Yourself.

Back in the mid-1970's, New York State decided to attract tourists with an "I Love New York" advertising campaign. The spokesperson for that campaign, Jane Maas, used this anecdote to open a speech:

"I was in Albany yesterday morning, having breakfast in the hotel coffee shop, and a cute little waitress spotted my button and came up to me and said, 'I'm from Georgia, but I *love* New York.' And I thought to myself, goodness, we are *living* the commercial."

Open with a Quotation.

Suppose you're giving a speech to honor your football coach. You could use a quotation like this:

"What makes a successful football team? Well, Bear Bryant said this is his secret. 'There's just three things I ever say. If anything goes bad, then I did it. If anything goes semi-good, then we did it. If anything goes real good, then you did it. That's all it takes to get people to win football games for you.'

"Our coach, Mr. Jones, uses that same secret, because he always makes us feel like a *team*, and that's why we want to give him this award tonight."

Use an Easy-to-Understand Definition.

Are you presenting a science project on chlorophyll? Try this opening:

"A few weeks ago, Mrs. Smith asked me to do a science project on something called 'chlorophyll.' I couldn't even *say* the word at first, and I *still* have trouble spelling it, but at least I now know what it means. Chlorophyll is the stuff that makes plants green."

Use a Real-Life Example.

Suppose you want the school administration to change the lunch schedule. You could say:

"Our lunch schedule doesn't work well. Our school has too many students to fit into just two lunch periods. We need to have three lunch periods so the lines won't be as crowded as they are right now.

"Let me give you some real-life examples: On Monday, I hurried to the lunch room as quickly as I could, and yet I still had to wait in line for seven minutes. On Tuesday, I had to return a book to the library before I went to lunch, and by the time I got to the cafeteria, the line was halfway across the floor. I had to wait for fifteen minutes because it was so crowded, and then I had to gulp down my food. This happens very often."

Use a Comparison.

Do you want to persuade the school board to let you enter a state-wide band competition? Then use a comparison like this:

"It's important for bands to compete in contests. That's the only way for band members to know how good they really are.

"Look at what other schools do. Penn High has entered three band competitions in the past ten years. And Wilson High has entered five. Yet we haven't entered any contests in the past ten years.

"Look at it this way: If we don't enter these contests, we can't win. And all of us band members would like to win so we could feel proud of the work we do here."

TELL THEM: THE BODY

Can you guess the most common mistake that people make with the body of their speech? They try to say *everything*, and so they wind up confusing (or boring!) their audience.

Don't let that happen to you. Stick to the one big topic you chose to talk about, and don't throw in any other material. Remember what I told you in Chapter Three: If you try to include *everything*, your listeners probably won't get *anything*.

It doesn't matter what you're talking about—a book report, a science project, a fund raising speech, whatever. You must focus your topic, and you must organize your material.

There are lots of ways to organize the body of your speech. Here are some ideas—use whichever one seems to work best for you.

Organize by Time.

Giving an oral book report? Tell the audience about the plot of the book in its natural time sequence: what happened first, what happened next, and so on.

Giving a presentation about your history project? Start by telling what happened in 1860, then 1861. . . .

Organize by Space.

Want to tell the audience about all the basketball courts in your town? Take it neighborhood by neighborhood.

Want to explain the battles in World War II? Take it country by country.

Want to report on the Girl Scout cookie sales for your county? Take it town by town.

By the way, a map can really help your audience follow this type of speech. You can point to France and talk about what went on there. Then you can point to Germany and talk about what went on there. You'll learn lots more about using maps (and other audio-visual aids) in Chapter Eight.

Use Alphabetical Order.

Do you have to give a treasurer's report for all the different clubs in your school? Talk about them in alphabetical order.

Do you want to give end-of-the-year awards to all of the athletic coaches in your school? Hand out those awards in alphabetical order.

Do you want to talk about all the volunteer projects that kids can help with in your community? Mention them in alphabetical order.

Use Cause-and-Effect Organization.

Want to talk about your science project? Start by telling what you did during your experiment, then talk about the results—the effects—of that action.

Want to talk about increased vandalism in your community? Explain that the lack of recreational activities causes teenagers to become bored and get into trouble.

Use Numerical Order.

Want to talk about your club's fund-raising projects this past year? Discuss them in numerical order: what project brought in the highest amount of money, the second highest amount of money, and so on down the line.

Take a Problem-Solution Approach.

Is there something wrong with your school's study-hall policy? Then tell your audience about that problem and offer some solutions.

For example: "Study hall is often a waste of time. Since we aren't allowed to go to the library during study hall, we don't have access to any of the reference books we need to do our work. So, we just sit there in study hall and waste our time. I'd like to propose a solution to this problem. . . ."

Use Psychological Order.

Dealing with a sensitive issue like nuclear power? Abortion rights? A ban on smoking in all public areas?

Think about the attitudes that your audience might have. If you think they will be hostile to your point of view, then you'd better ease slowly into your speech.

What do you think your listeners would find most acceptable? Most important? Most interesting? Put that up front. Don't alienate your audience by starting with controversial information that will upset them. Start on common ground, and then ease into your position.

TELL THEM WHAT YOU TOLD THEM: THE CONCLUSION

All right, you've given them the guts of the speech. You've said everything that needs to be said on your particular topic—or, at least, everything that you have time for in one short speech!

Now's the time to wrap it up—nice and clean. Don't stick in any new thoughts, or add another statistic, or say, "Oh, just one more thing. . . ."

When you get to the end of your speech, your listeners won't want to hear "just one more thing." They will want you to sum up your message simply and directly.

Your ending may be the only thing your audience remembers, so be sure to make it interesting. How can you give them a good ending? Here are some ways that have worked for me and many other speakers:

End with an Anecdote.

Suppose you're trying to raise money for starving children in Africa. You could end this way:

"Maybe you're thinking to yourselves, 'Yes, I really do feel sorry for those starving kids, but what can I do? I'm just one small person.'

"Well, I'd like to end by telling you about a conversation that President Theodore Roosevelt had almost ninety years ago.

"President Roosevelt was speaking to an audience in the midwest about a crisis that was facing the country. When he finished his talk, someone in that audience came up to him and said, 'Mr. President, I'm just an ordinary businessman. What can I possibly do to help?'

"And do you know what Teddy Roosevelt told that man? He told him, 'Do what you can—with what you've got—where you are. But do it!'"

End with Optimism.

When Ted Kennedy lost the Democratic nomination for president back in 1980, he didn't speak with bitterness.

He spoke with optimism. Here is how he ended his concession speech:

"For me, a few hours ago, this campaign came to an end. For all those whose cares have been our concern, the work goes on, the cause endures, the hope still lives and the dream shall never die."

End by Referring to a Popular Song or a Popular Movie.

Are you trying to get kids to volunteer at a senior citizens center? Make an emotional appeal:

"I'm asking you to give your time and your energy and your enthusiasm to this cause. But, most of all, I'm asking you to give your love.

"You know, twenty-five years ago—long before any of us was even born—the hit song in America was called, 'What The World Needs Now Is Love, Sweet Love.'

"Well, what the world needs now is still love, sweet love. And it's up to us to share our love with all the older people in our town who need us so very much."

Refer to the Opening of Your Speech.

President Reagan used this conclusion when he spoke to the United Nations:

"I began these remarks speaking of our children. I want to close on the same theme. Our children should not grow up frightened. They should not fear the future. . . .

"Let us reaffirm America's destiny of goodness and good will. Let us work for peace; and as we do, let us remember the lines of the famous old hymn, 'O God of Love, O King of Peace/Make wars throughout the world to cease.'"

End with a Quotation.

Do you want to honor the hockey team for winning the state championship? An ending like this would work:

"Eddie Rickenbacker, the famous pilot, once said, 'I can give you a six-word formula for success: 'Think things through—then follow through.'

"That's what your team has done this year. That's why you're so successful. And that's why we're honoring you tonight."

End with a Proverb.

Do you want to encourage your audience to stick in there and keep trying? Consider an ending like this:

"Yes, it's been a tough job. And, no, we won't be able to solve our problems overnight. But, we've got to hang in there. We've got to keep trying.

"There's an old proverb that says, 'The best fish are near the bottom.' So, let's not get discouraged. Our reward is coming."

7

HUMOR
(OR HOW TO GET A
CHUCKLE WITHOUT
STICKING YOUR FOOT
IN YOUR MOUTH)

So, you're in the middle of your speech, and you notice that everyone looks bored. You think, "Maybe I should come up with a funny joke to make them laugh and make them like me."

Well, maybe not! I'm sorry to say that jokes can backfire. Why? Because most speakers don't use humor properly. They tell jokes that are either insulting, or just plain silly.

How can you tell a joke without sticking your foot in your mouth? Ask yourself these five questions before you decide to use a joke:

1. Will this joke fit into the mood of my speech? (A serious speech about child abuse or world hunger or teenage suicide would be destroyed by a silly joke.)
2. Will my audience feel comfortable with this joke? (Go back and reread Chapter Four, then think about your audience very carefully. Make sure they will think your joke is amusing, not annoying.)
3. Is this joke short? (Long jokes are hard for speakers to tell, and hard for listeners to follow.)
4. Is the joke fresh? (If you've heard the joke twice in the past week, your audience has probably heard it, too. Nothing's worse than a joke with a stale punch line!)
5. Can I deliver this joke really well? (Let's face it: not all of us can tell a joke the way it's *meant* to be told.)

If you can't honestly answer "yes" to all of these questions—well, just skip the joke. It's better *not* to tell a joke than to tell a joke that makes *you* look silly. If you can answer yes, here are some ideas of how to go about finding the right one.

WHERE CAN YOU FIND HUMOR?

Ask your librarian to show you the humor section, and

take a few minutes to browse around. You'll probably find a few books that contain jokes. These books can be helpful, but *only* if you make the material sound natural—as if it really happened to you.

I prefer to make up my own funny stories based on experiences that have really happened to me or my family or friends.

What makes personalized jokes better? Three big reasons:

1. Since I've created my own humorous touches, I can be sure this joke will be fresh to my audience.
2. Since the humor comes from my own personal experience, it will be easier for me to deliver and it will sound more natural.
3. Since I'm sharing something personal with my audience, they will feel more friendly to me.

WHAT'S THE SAFEST KIND OF HUMOR?

The safest kind of humor is the kind that pokes a little bit of fun at *yourself*. The most dangerous kind of humor is the kind that makes fun of *other* people—other countries, other religions, other age groups, other races, other high schools, other teachers, et cetera.

Why? Again, three big reasons:

1. Because you never know exactly who will be in your audience. You may make a nasty wisecrack about another country, and someone in your audience could have a parent who was born in that country.
2. Because your audience will get nervous. They'll think, "If he's making fun of all *those* people,

maybe he'll wind up making fun of me, too."

3. Because it's just plain NOT NICE to make cruel jokes about other people. You wouldn't like it if people made fun of you, and your religion, your family, your hometown, would you???

Here's how some famous people have poked gentle fun at themselves:

- A little boy once asked John F. Kennedy how he became a war hero. "It was absolutely involuntary," Kennedy said. "They sank my boat."
- People used to tease Senator John Glenn about being dull. So when the Senator spoke at a big dinner in Washington, he mocked his own reputation for being dull: "I am not dull. Boring, maybe, but not dull."

HOW EASILY CAN YOU GET A LAUGH?

Sometimes it's almost impossible to get a laugh—no matter how funny your joke is. If people are preoccupied with something else, they won't feel like playing around.

For example, if you're speaking early in the morning, the audience may be too sleepy to appreciate your humor. I've found that it's usually easier to get a laugh as the day goes on. That's because people are more awake later in the day and more willing to sit back and relax. (If you don't believe me, think about how groggy and grouchy *you* are first thing in the morning!)

Of course, sometimes it's *too late* for humor to work. Suppose you're speaking just before lunchtime— or just before school closes at the end of the day. Your listeners will be impatient to get out and meet their friends. If you tell long-winded jokes and cause them to be late, they will resent you. So, beware!

A FEW WORDS OF CAUTION ABOUT JOKES THAT *NEVER* WORK

Some jokes never work in a speech. Racial jokes. Ethnic jokes. Dirty jokes. Jokes that make fun of old age. Jokes that make fun of a handicap. Jokes that make fun of drunkenness.

These jokes will backfire, so don't use them. *Ever.*

You might think it's funny to make a joke about drunk drivers, but if someone in your audience had a mother who was killed by a drunk driver . . . well, that person won't think your joke is very funny.

You might think it's funny to make jokes about little old men and little old ladies who always do silly things. Well, it *isn't* funny. Old people were once young people, just like you. They don't like to be made fun of just because they've grown older.

You might also think it's funny to make jokes about blind people or deaf people. Well, blind people and deaf people have feelings, just like you. If you suddenly lost your sight or your hearing, would you like people to mock you?

A member of President Ford's administration, Earl Butz, once made a tacky joke about the Pope. People were offended by Mr. Butz's sense of humor, and he was eventually forced to resign.

Later, a member of President Reagan's administration, James Watt, made a nasty joke about "cripples." Again people were offended by his tasteless sense of humor, and he was also forced to resign.

So avoid stupid jokes. Don't stick your foot in your mouth.

THE NITTY-GRITTY DETAILS

AUDIO-VISUAL AIDS

There's an old saying: A picture is worth a thousand words. That certainly applies to many presentations. If you use audio-visual aids well, your audience will probably get a lot more out of your message.

Unfortunately, a lot of people don't use these aids well. In fact, A-V aids ruin more speeches than they improve. Why? Because most people don't take the time to prepare good material.

If you turn to the appendix at the end of this book, you'll learn about many different kinds of A-V aids you can use when you give a presentation:

- blackboards
- posters
- flannel boards
- cork bulletin boards
- flip charts
- objects to hold up and talk about
- slide projectors
- films
- videotapes
- tape recorders
- radios

All of these A-V aids have their advantages and their disadvantages. Choose the one that works best with your material—and that you feel most comfortable with.

HOW TO PREPARE GOOD NOTES

Let's suppose you have to talk about nuclear war to your social studies class. Your teacher asks you to speak for a full ten minutes.

How will you ever be able to memorize all of that material? Easy—you don't have to memorize all of that material. You can use notes to jog your memory.

Good notes have to meet three requirements:

1. They should contain enough information to

help you remember the important points of your speech.

2. They should be easy for you to use.

3. And they should not distract the audience.

Many speakers like to put their notes on 3×5 index cards. These are small enough to fit into your hand or a pocket, and so you can carry them to the podium without anybody noticing them.

Other speakers need to use bigger index cards: perhaps 4×6 or 5×7. If you must refer to a lot of statistics or quotations, you will probably need the extra space of these bigger cards. (Also, if your handwriting is large, or if your vision is not good, these bigger cards will make things easier for you.)

Of course, you can't hide large-size note cards in the palm of your hand—or even in most pockets. But, don't worry about that. Just secure them neatly with a paper clip, hold them firmly in one hand as you walk to the podium, and no one will be distracted.

What should you put on your note cards? Use key phrases to remind you of the major sections of your speech. Also write down any statistics or any quotations.

A sample card might look like this:

1971 — What Happened?
Hit song: "I'd like to Teach
    the World to Sing"
Best comedy actor: Alan Alda
    for "MASH"
Nobel Peace Prize: Willy Brandt

How many cards can you use? The answer will depend on you. If it's a simple speech and you know the material very well, one or two cards might be enough. But if it's a long speech and it has a lot of details, you might have to use as many as a dozen note cards. (Be careful, though. If you use *too* many cards, they will become a crutch. They will distract you, as well as the audience.)

Always be sure to number the order of your cards. That way, if you accidentally drop them before your speech, you can be sure you're putting them back in the correct order.

Never staple your note cards together. Instead, use a large paper clip. When you get to the podium, simply remove the paper clip and you're ready to go. As you finish with each card, slide it to the side quietly—don't flip the cards over because such a noisy movement distracts the audience.

WHEN DO YOU NEED TO WRITE THE WHOLE SPEECH?

For most informal presentations, note cards are just fine. But there are times when you will want to write out your whole speech:

- when it's a very important occasion and you need to make every word count
- when time is strictly limited and you must be absolutely certain of staying within your allotted sixty-second or ninety-second time frame
- when people from the press might be quoting you
- when you are feeling particularly anxious about forgetting portions of your speech and want the security of having a fully prepared manuscript

If you decide to write out the full speech, use these ten guidelines to guarantee a smooth delivery:

1. Type it in large letters so you can read it easily.
2. Double-space between lines. Triple-space between paragraphs.
3. Never hyphenate words at the ends of lines. It's better to leave the line short rather than hyphenate.
4. End each page with a complete sentence. (It's too dangerous to start a sentence on one page and finish it on another. You would lose too much time while shifting the page, and your delivery would sound stilted.)
5. Type only on the top ⅔ of the page. Leave the bottom ⅓ of the page blank. (Why? Because if you try reading a speech that runs all the way to the bottom of the page, your head will bend down too far, the audience won't be able to see your face, and your voice will sound muffled.)
6. Leave wide margins all around the edges of the page.
7. Number each page. (Upper right is usually the best place.)
8. Underline any words or phrases you want to emphasize.
9. Never staple the pages of your speech together. Fasten them with a paper clip, which is easy to remove when you're ready to speak.
10. Place the manuscript in a plain folder—ready for you to deliver.

One last word to the wise:
Always prepare an extra copy of your speech and

keep it in a separate place. (For example, if you carry one copy in your school bag, keep another copy in your locker or in your teacher's filing cabinet. Even if you lose one copy, the show can still go on.)

9
HOW TO CONTROL YOUR NERVOUSNESS

- A stomach that feels like it's doing flip-flops.
- A heart that pounds.
- A mouth that gets dry.
- Hands that shake.
- Legs that wobble when you walk.

These are all signs of nervousness.

The bad news is that nervousness affects almost every speaker . . . not just young people, but adults, too. The good news is that you can learn to control your nervousness so it doesn't bother you or your audience.

If you start to feel nervous a couple of days before your speech, don't feel embarrassed. Everyone feels that way before a speech.

In fact, the medical school at the University of Ohio did a survey, and they found that people are more afraid of speaking in public than almost anything else. It's scarier than going on a blind date or playing a championship game or facing a job interview, for example.

What can you do about these scary feelings? Lots of things.

You can start by understanding what nervousness is. Nervousness is simply energy. If you control that energy, you can make it work for you. You can use the extra energy to give a better, livelier speech.

But if you allow that energy to run wild—if you allow it to control you—then you'll have problems.

Here are some tricks of the trade that professional speakers use to prevent nervousness. (Yes, even professional speakers get nervous. They just learn to control it better than most of us.)

TRY PHYSICAL EXERCISES

1. Play some baseball or go for a swim or take your dog on a long run the day before you speak. If you keep your body active, it will be too busy to get nervous.

2. Go to the bathroom an hour before you speak. (Most people need to use the toilet when they get nervous, so be sure to allow some extra time for this.)

3. Just before you speak, go off by yourself to an empty room and do some jumping jacks or run in place. Let off steam! (But, don't exercise too much or you'll get hot and sweaty. Just move around for twenty or thirty seconds. That should be enough.)

4. Make funny faces. Puff up your cheeks, then let the air escape. (Of course, you will look silly doing this, so do it where no one can see you. Again, the bathroom is a good place for these private exercises.)

5. Make more funny faces. Open your mouth and your eyes wide, then close them tightly.

6. Yawn slowly a few times. This will loosen your jaw and help to clear your throat.

7. Concentrate on the part of your body that feels most tense. Your stomach, maybe? Or your hands? Deliberately tighten that part even more until it starts to quiver, then let go. You will feel much more relaxed. Repeat this a couple of times.

8. Swing your arms in front of you. Do the right arm, then the left arm, then both arms together.

9. Pretend you're an opera singer. Try singing "mi, mi, mi." Be dramatic and wave your arms as you do it. (You may want to flush the toilet during this exercise to cover up the sounds!)

TRY MENTAL EXERCISES

1. Think about something that's given you good memories. (Maybe fishing with your brother on a cool mountain lake. Or playing volleyball with friends on a sandy beach.) Try to remember how wonderful you felt doing that.

2. Imagine something you'd like to learn to do. (Sailing, for example.) Draw a picture of that activity in your mind. Be as specific as possible. Really see the sailboat, the waves on the ocean, the color of your clothes. Feel the excitement of mastering that activity.

3. Water often makes people feel calm. Turn on the bathroom faucet and close your eyes and just daydream for a minute. Let the sound of the water relax you.

TRY THINKING POSITIVELY

1. Say to yourself, "I'm prepared. I read this book carefully. I can give a good book report."

2. Or say, "I worked on this science project for three weeks. No one knows as much about this science project as me."

3. Or say, "I'm glad I have a chance to do this oral history report for extra credit. It will help my grade go up from a C to a B."

4. Or say, "I don't love giving speeches, but I'd rather give a speech than write a ten-page report."

5. Or say, "If I had to choose between giving a speech and cleaning my parent's basement, I guess I'd rather give a speech."

6. Or think of something that's *really* frightening—getting an F in English, or losing your allowance, or getting grounded at home. Giving a speech should start to look good by comparison!

TRY A TEST RUN

1. Do what good athletes do—try a test run and see yourself as a winner.

For example, here is what one U.S. Olympic athlete imagined before she ran the luge race: "You close your eyes and think about every inch of the course and what you are going to do . . . You think about the start and each curve, where you are going to enter a curve, where you will leave the curve. You run the race in your mind all the way to the bottom of the hill. It's amazingly accurate."

2. Use this same technique to "see" exactly what will happen when you give your speech. Close your eyes and say to yourself:

• "Okay, when the teacher calls on me, I'll push back my seat, stand up and pick up my notes from the top of my desk.

• Then I'll stand up straight, make sure my hair is out of my eyes, and walk briskly to the front of the room.

• When I get up there, I'll put my notes on the podium and make sure they're in the right order.

• I'll plant both feet firmly on the ground and take a deep breath. Then I'll look at the class for a second before I begin to talk so I can get their attention.

• If people are rustling papers (or if Johnny Shannon is rocking his chair back and forth like he always does), I'll wait an extra second or two for everyone to quiet down before I begin to speak.

• My voice will be friendly and relaxed and strong, and people will like listening to what I say. . . ."

Imagine the entire speech as carefully as you can. Visualize as many details as possible. If you see yourself as successful during this test run, you will be successful when you actually give your speech.

PICK AND CHOOSE

Well, I've just given you lots of practical tips to help

control nervousness. Do you have to use *all* of them? Of course not!

Try a couple of these suggestions each time you speak, and see how well they work for you. Some will work better than others—you pick the ones that work best for you.

10
THE COUNTDOWN

Okay, you've done all the right things. You've focused your topic, thought about your audience, come up with interesting research. You've organized your material so it's easy to follow, and now you're ready to give your speech.

Well, not quite. You're *almost* ready, but you still have one more thing to do: PRACTICE!

Athletes have to practice if they want to be good. Musicians have to practice if they want to be good. Cooks, race car drivers, carpenters . . . they all have to practice. Speakers are no exception.

Practice your delivery in four stages:

1. START BY GIVING THE SPEECH ALOUD TO YOURSELF.

Use the notes to help you remember what comes next. (Feel free to look at your notes often the first few times you rehearse.)

Tape record the speech. See how long it takes. Listen—really *listen*—to your voice. Is it clear, or do you tend to drop your voice at the end of each sentence?

Do you speak too fast? (Most people speak about 150 words per minute. You might want to get a stop watch, speak for one minute, and count the number of words you said.)

Is your voice loud enough? If you usually have trouble speaking up, try putting the tape recorder across the room while you practice. This should *force* you to speak louder.

2. DELIVER THE SPEECH STANDING IN FRONT OF A MIRROR.

After you've gone through the speech a few times, you

shouldn't have to use your notes too much. Look up. Smile. Notice how your face becomes more lively at certain points in your speech—when you're telling a funny story, for example, or talking about something really unusual.

BE CAREFUL: Practice the entire speech each time you go through it. Otherwise you'll have a great beginning but a weak ending. If you make a mistake during your delivery, don't go back and start over again. Just keep on going. That's what you would do in front of a real audience—and that's what you should do during practice sessions.

3. DELIVER THE SPEECH IN FRONT OF A FRIEND.

Okay, you might feel a little bit funny doing this, but you might as well get used to it because soon—on Speech-Day!—you'll have to give the speech in front of lots of other people. The sooner you get used to an audience, the better off you'll be.

Pick a friend who won't do silly things like make faces at you or try to crack you up. If all of your friends do silly things like that, then ask a parent or a neighbor or a teacher to watch you rehearse.

Pretend this is for real. Plant your feet firmly and stand up straight. Use a lectern for your notes (or a table, if you don't have a lectern handy). Practice sliding the notecards quietly from side to side—remember, don't flip them over because that's too distracting to your audience.

Use good eye contact—really *look* at your listener. Smile when it feels natural. Gesture with your hand to make a point.

4. PRACTICE BEFORE A SMALL GROUP.

To be honest, you don't have to bother with this step all of the time. But, if you're nervous about speaking and want some extra practice—or if you're giving a really important speech and want to be as good as possible—then you should do a run-through in front of a few people.

So arrange a few chairs and have a trial run. Try to make good eye contact with each person. Play with your voice a little bit. Go faster, slower, louder, softer—whatever it takes to keep your audience interested.

It's best if you can practice in the room where you will actually speak. But if you can't do that, at least make sure you check out the room in advance to make sure you're comfortable with the layout. If you're speaking out of town, ask to see a sketch of the room. Just knowing what the room will look like will make you feel more in control—and help reduce any nervousness.

WHAT THEY SEE IS WHAT THEY GET

Some people think that a speech starts when they actually begin to talk. These people are wrong. A speech starts as soon as you enter the room.

Your audience will start to form an opinion of you as soon as they see you. First impressions really do count, so be sure to make yours good.

Let them see a well-groomed person. Comb your hair or put on your lipstick *before* you enter the room . . . no last-minute grooming in public, please.

In fact, make it a point to check yourself in the mirror before every speech. You'll prevent lots of disasters this way. (A businessman I know once forgot to do this—and he wound up being very embarrassed when he later found out that a long piece of spinach had gotten stuck in his teeth and was hanging from the corner of his mouth during his speech! He now carries a toothbrush in his briefcase at all times and uses it just before a speech—a good rule for you to follow, too.)

As you walk to the front of the room to give your speech, everyone will be looking at you, so try to look cool, calm and collected. (In other words, don't be chewing your nails or tucking your shirt into your pants, or shuffling with your note cards.)

When you get to the front of the room, place your notes on a lectern or a table. Stand straight and place your weight evenly over both feet—this will help you feel in control of the situation and prevent rocking back and forth.

Take a good look at the audience before you begin to speak. This pause will give them time to stop shuffling their chairs and talking. It will also give you a chance to breathe. Now, you're ready to speak.

When you finish speaking the last word of your presentation, don't rush off. Your speech isn't really finished yet. Hold your position and look directly at the audience for a few more seconds. Let your ending sink in.

Then gather your notes and walk away from the podium. Walk briskly and with confidence—the same way you approached the podium.

When you get back to your seat, don't start talking to the person next to you. Someone else—maybe your teacher—is at the front of the room right now, and it would be rude for you to be talking.

Above all, avoid saying stuff like, "Boy, did I ever mess that one up," or "Wow, am I glad *that's* over!"

Those are sure ways to detract from an otherwise good speech.

Just sit there quietly, looking attentive and confident.

Who knows? You may even get applause. If that happens, smile and look pleased.

After all, what could be better than having an audience love what you did? You put a lot of work into preparing a good speech—now sit back and enjoy all the good comments that will come your way!

AUDIO VISUAL AIDS

BLACKBOARDS

Advantages:

- every classroom has one
- they don't take up any floor space
- they're easy to erase and change
- they're big, so lots of people can see them
- you can keep adding things to the blackboard as you talk (so you don't have to reveal everything at once—perfect for math or science formulas, for example)
- it gives you something to do with your hands
- you can ask the audience a question and then put some of their thoughts on the blackboard (people love to see their own ideas written in big letters—it makes them feel important)

Disadvantages:

- you have to turn your back to the audience when you write (so you lose valuable eye contact with your listeners)
- if your penmanship is poor, the audience won't be able to read what you write

- if you don't write large enough, the audience won't even be able to see what's on the blackboard
- it's hard to write and talk at the same time
- you might accidentally erase something
- you might misspell a word
- you might make the chalk squeak
- you'll probably get chalk dust all over your clothes

Tips:

- use soft chalk, not hard
- if you have any choice, pick a green blackboard and use a soft yellow chalk (easier on the eyes than white chalk on a dark blackboard)
- learn to draw a straight line (Hint: It's just like playing a sport. *You have to keep your eye on the ball.* Put your chalk wherever you want the line to begin, then stare at the spot where you want it to end. Keep looking at this end spot while you move the chalk firmly. Miracle! You'll draw a straight line!)
- also, learn to keep your letters level (Hint: Practice makes perfect.)
- if you want to shade an area, use the side of the chalk stick

POSTERS

Advantages:

- you can make them in advance (and avoid those last-minute mistakes.)
- they're inexpensive to make
- they can be colorful

Disadvantages:

- they may not be large enough to get your message across
- they can be awkward to carry around all day

Tips:

- give each poster a title
- keep it simple (only one illustration per poster)
- make your letters big enough
- don't squash the space
- Complementary colors (red/green, yellow/purple, orange/blue) produce the greatest contrast, but they have a bad side-effect—sometimes the sharp contrast will make the colors seem to vibrate. (Use soft pastel colors for the most pleasing effect.)
- store your posters safely in a closet until it's time for you to speak (you'll avoid that dog-eared look, and you'll prevent people from taking sneak-peeks).

FLANNEL BOARDS

Advantages:

- fun for you to work with
- since they aren't very common, audiences may like the novelty
- can be very colorful
- good for showing how things move around (traffic patterns, planetary orbits, et cetera)

Disadvantages:

- too bulky to carry around
- too small to show to large groups (If you have more than ten people, they won't even be able to see the board.)

- humidity can prevent proper sticking
- a rough jolt can make the pieces fall off
- the background flannel wears thin

Tips:

- make your felt pieces large enough for people to see and simple enough for them to understand
- move your pieces slowly, so people can follow you
- make sure each piece sticks

CORK BULLETIN BOARDS

Advantages:

- almost every classroom has one
- large enough for you to make a really creative display
- nothing to carry around
- cheap to use

Disadvantages:

- since you must prepare the bulletin board in advance, people will look at it before you give your presentation, and this will take away some of the suspense of your message
- also, since it's in public space, it might suffer from graffiti or other vandalism

Tips:

- try to put up your display as close to the delivery of your speech as possible (to minimize graffiti and vandalism)
- take advantage of all that space by using big letters for your titles and big illustrations

FLIP CHARTS

Advantages:

• cheap
• can be prepared in advance, or written during your presentation
• better than blackboards because each sheet can be saved for future reference
• you can give handouts of the charts by writing their content on standard-sized typing paper and making duplicate copies

Disadvantages:

• if you write on the flip chart while you speak, your penmanship might be illegible

Tips:

• use a felt-tip marker with a wide stroke
• make sure the ink is fresh and dark enough for all to see

OBJECTS TO HOLD UP AND TALK ABOUT

Advantages:

• can give the audience a real-life view of something
• can help people understand just how something works

Disadvantages:

• only works with very small groups of people (say, a half dozen or so); otherwise, no one can see what you're holding up

- if people try to handle the object while you're speaking, they will get distracted and won't pay attention to your message

Tips:

- hold up the object long enough for everyone to get a good look (be sure to turn it around so they can see all sides)
- offer to let people handle the object after you've finished speaking

SLIDE SHOWS

Advantages:

- a picture that's projected onto a big screen is always more dramatic than smaller illustrations
- you can show real-life shots of people

Disadvantages:

- when you turn the lights off, some of your listeners may not bother to listen any more (beware of spit balls and the passing of love notes)
- if the machine breaks down, people will get restless

Tips:

- double-check all slides to make sure they are in the proper order (you know how annoyed you get when you have to watch a slide show where half the slides are in upside down!)
- tape down the projector cord so no one will trip on it
- make the room as dark as possible
- use a screen, not the wall

FILMS

Advantages:

• everyone loves a film!
• some things you can *show* much better than you can describe (for example: foreign countries, slow-motion operations of machinery, historical events)

Disadvantages:

• you might not have enough time to show a film *and* give a speech
• if the film breaks in the middle, you'll hear a lot of "boo's"

Tips:

• ask your librarian for good sources of free films
• be sure to have a full run-through of the film in advance

VIDEOTAPES

Advantages:

• everyone loves a TV show!
• easier to show than a film

Disadvantages:

• the TV screen may not be big enough for every-one to see
• video quality may not be as good as film quality

Tips:

• check each TV monitor in advance
• make sure the volume is properly adjusted

TAPE RECORDERS

Advantages:

- easy to carry around
- cheap (tapes are reusable)
- ideal for presenting a new radio jingle, or playing a hit song that ties in with your message, or sharing comments from experts you've interviewed while researching your speech

Disadvantages:

- batteries can get weak
- if the tape runs too long, listeners will get restless because they don't have anything to look at

Tips:

- practice playing the tape several times so you're familiar with all the buttons
- carry extra batteries

RADIOS

Advantages:

- great if you're talking about advertising (you can turn on the radio and play a few live commercials for the audience)
- great if you're giving a report for your music class (you can turn on the radio to show different kinds of music: rock, pop, jazz, classical, easy listening)
- great if you're giving a report for a social studies class (you can tune in to an all-news station and hear history in the making)

Disadvantages:

• static
• can't be sure exactly what will be playing at what time

Tips:

• be sure you know *exactly* how to tune in each station
• if your speech is from 11:00 A.M. to 11:15 A.M., listen to the radio station during that time slot for several days in advance so you know what to expect

A FEW WORDS ABOUT CHARTS

For some presentations, you might want to use charts. Charts are easy to prepare, and they can make a great impression on an audience. (What's more, they can make a great impression on *teachers*, which can be pretty important if you're looking for a good grade.)

Of course, you have to come up with *good looking* charts. Here are some practical tips:

The Pie Chart

1. Don't use more than five or six parts in a pie chart. Otherwise, your chart will look too cluttered.
2. Always put the most important section at the top of the pie. (Why? Because our eyes are used to looking at clocks, and we tend to see things in a clockwise motion.)
3. If you have one section that's more important than the others, use color to make that section stand out. (Maybe hot pink against a black background— that should catch their attention!)

4. Working in just black and white? Then make the most important section stand out by giving it the darkest shade.

5. Give the chart a title.

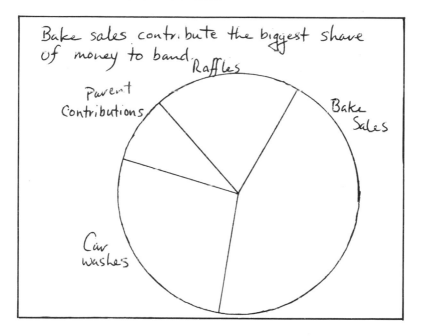

Bake sales contribute the biggest share of money to band.

Raffles

Parent Contributions

Bake Sales

Car washes

The Bar Chart

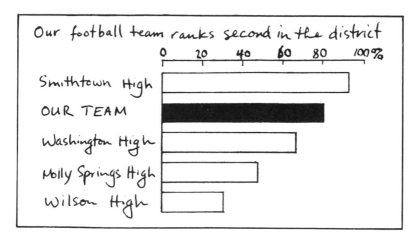

Our football team ranks second in the district

0   20   40   60   80   100%

Smithtown High

OUR TEAM

Washington High

Holly Springs High

Wilson High

1. Make sure that the space between the bars is smaller than the bars.

2. Use color or shading to show off the most important bar.

3. Either use numbers at the top of the scale OR numbers at the end of the bars . . . BUT NOT BOTH PLACES (that would be too cluttered).

4. Round out the numbers. (Say $100, instead of $101.45)

The Column Chart

1. This is a great way to show how things change over a period of time.

2. Follow the basic rules that apply to bar charts.

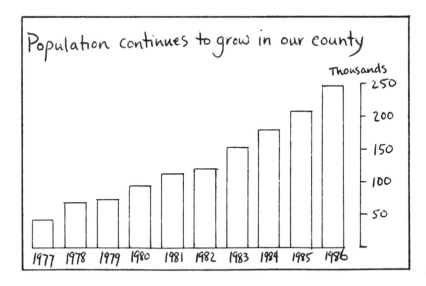

The Line Chart

1. If you need to use two lines, use different colors to distinguish them. (Or, if you're working in black and white, make the most important line very bold and use short dashes for the other line.)

2. Try not to use more than three lines, or else you will have a chart that looks like a plate full of spaghetti.

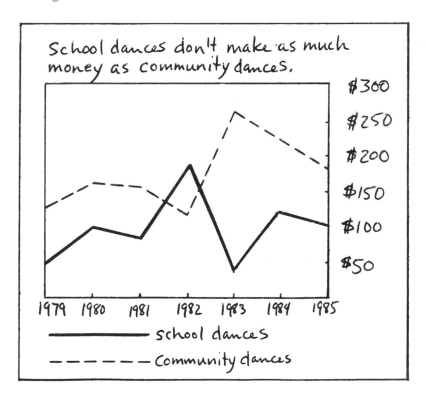

School dances don't make as much money as community dances.

$300
$250
$200
$150
$100
$50

1979 1980 1981 1982 1983 1984 1985

———— School dances
— — — — Community dances

The Spaghetti Chart

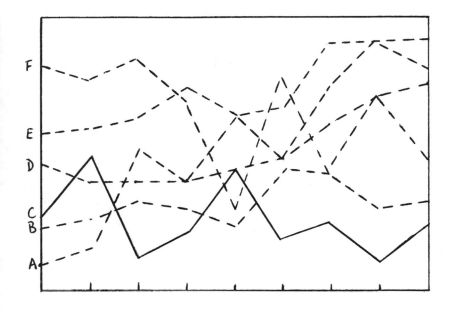

INDEX